YOUR KNOWLEDGE HAS VALUE

- We will publish your bachelor's and master's thesis, essays and papers

- Your own eBook and book - sold worldwide in all relevant shops

- Earn money with each sale

Upload your text at www.GRIN.com and publish for free

Silva Tony

The consequences of modernization in Siam

GRIN Verlag

Bibliografische Information der Deutschen Nationalbibliothek:

Die Deutsche Bibliothek verzeichnet diese Publikation in der Deutschen National-
bibliografie; detaillierte bibliografische Daten sind im Internet über http://dnb.d-
nb.de/ abrufbar.

Imprint:

Copyright © 2013 GRIN Verlag GmbH
Druck und Bindung: Books on Demand GmbH, Norderstedt Germany
ISBN: 978-3-656-63809-4

This book at GRIN:

http://www.grin.com/en/e-book/271566/the-consequences-of-modernization-in-
siam

GRIN - Your knowledge has value

Der GRIN Verlag publiziert seit 1998 wissenschaftliche Arbeiten von Studenten, Hochschullehrern und anderen Akademikern als eBook und gedrucktes Buch. Die Verlagswebsite www.grin.com ist die ideale Plattform zur Veröffentlichung von Hausarbeiten, Abschlussarbeiten, wissenschaftlichen Aufsätzen, Dissertationen und Fachbüchern.

Visit us on the internet:

http://www.grin.com/

http://www.facebook.com/grincom

http://www.twitter.com/grin_com

Introduction

The world is currently plagued with inequality and exploitation. Several movements have been established across the globe to preach peace, social justice and ecological sustainability. We often come across inspiring stories of individuals or groups utilizing their ingenuity in ensuring social justice and environmental protection. Sivaraksa in his book *Conflict, Culture, Change: Engaged Buddhism in a Globalizing World* notes that modernization is the root source of cultural erosion amongst the people of Siam. According to Sivaraksa, modernization has come with lack of respect for nature, social justice and equality (Sivaraksa 107).

Sivaraksa fends for the survival of his tradition – Buddhism. In essence, Sivaraksa is not entirely opposed to modernization; rather, he observes that the modernization process can also borrow from the sustainable traditional approaches. He is keen to select from and rebuild Buddhism in a quest for the traditional roots of his religion. Sivaraksa identifies the complex and ambiguous nature of modernity, and asserts the need to embrace the spirit of Buddhism in its traditional form (43).

Sivaraksa relates the modern history of Siam to that of Thai during the Western Imperialism. Even though King Mongkut employed several diplomatic efforts to defend Thai from foreign dominance, the Westren imperialists developed new reforms that saw a change in the culture, administrative structure, educational system and even the military structure. As a result of the elite's leadership, Siam grew so fast to become more like a Western center. During King Rama's reign, western culture dominated the lifestyles of the Siam people. As Sivaraksa notes, "life in the countryside was negatively impacted" (109). This period saw a lot of change in the traditional ways of life as people were even forces to emulate the western mode of lifestyle.

The Consequences of Modernization in Siam

Thai's elites, such as King Rama V, through imitation of the Western concept of modernization, facilitated the seperation between the past and the present – traditional culture and modern culture. Sivaraksa further argues that even the Buddhist tradition was no exception in the departure towards modernity. The Thai elites subjected Buddhism to the test of modern science. In his view, modernity is concealed behind the masks of development and globalization, whereas it is a powerful tool used by Western states such as the United States to attain global dominance at the expense of places such as Siam.

Sivaraksa shows how Siam and other parts of the world are subjects of. Greed, hatred and ignorance dominate the modern Siam capitalism against the Buddhist ideal of selflessness. He subscribes to the perception that modernism has led to the spirit of individualism as people get obsessed with material gains. People in Siam are fast adopting the luxurious lifestyle where suffering and stress are kept at bay. The spirit of solidarity and communism among peasants is slowly fading amidst the forces of market competition (107).

Siam in its traditional set up, before modernism cropped in, placed high value on natural resources, and had high respect for life. During this time, Buddhist monks employed non-violent and spiritual tactics to protect the forests against any form of destruction. However, with globalization, the industrial revolution coupled with mass technological inventions has seen destruction of forested land in many parts across the globe. Modernization is responsible for the destruction of nature (108).

Sivaraksa blames modernization for overexploitation of natural resources, as well as, the gap between the rich and the poor. In his own understanding, the developed states, such as United States, have unleashed economic forces upon the developing states which often result in deteroriated living conditions. He uses the example of United States invasion of Afghanistan to explain the oppression that faces the Afghan citizens who had nothin to do with the 9/11 (8). The quest for equality is now guided by money and power (109).

In order to illustrate the suffering associated with capitalism, Sivaraksa focuses on Siam. He uses the example of international treaties demonstrate the effect of economic oppression affects the local people. Several development initiatives have resulted into foreign dominance in the Siam market. Faced with competition, it's so had to make a reasonable livelihood. Developemnt has also been responsible for eretion of modern buildings which consume a lot of space initially occupied by trees and other natural resources.

Sivaraksa depicts how modernization or capitalism has reduced Siam people to become desire-driven people. Spaces initially occupied by Buddhist temples now harbour commercial stores. He notes that consumerism is responsible for global monoculture with technological, fast food, and junk food dominance. Adverts ar used to lure people to acquire material goods without contentment. Some of the goods are used to attain social status or glamour often

2

resulting to more greed for money and power. In Siam, there's stiff competition towards acquisition of wealth making people t abandon the traditional ways of life (113).

Sivaraksi's Response to the Challenges of Modernization

In order to level the global forces responsible for capitalism, we must embrace the traditional Buddhist teachings. According to Sivaraksa, spiritual development of wisdom and compassion is the main challenge facing the world. He uses the Buddhist perception to link the suffering facing the world to greed, hatred and delusion. Capitalism and consumerism, in his view is dominated by greed (115).

In order to overcome the 'evils' of capitalism and consumerism, the Siam people must abandon the western luxurious lifestyles and embrace suffering as enshrined in the Buddist tradition. Civilization or luxurious forms of lifestyle is an obstacle to peace and happiness. The Siam people must adopt the spirit of solidarity and communism in order to ensure social justice and equality among themselves (112).

Additionally, respect for nature results into freedom from want and deprivation. Nature supplies all the basic needs – food, shelter, clothing and medicine. The people should opt for traditional forms of lifestyle, where nature has a high value in the society. The Siam people should ape the indigenous Budhist Monks who did anything to protect forests (107).

The movie *Buddha's Lost Children* is in line with Savaraksi's advocacy for true suffering in the spirit of sourcing for social justice, peace and equality. In the movie, Khru Bah – a kickboxing champion – fights for the rights of orphaned children from rural parts of Thailand. Khru Bah demonstrates the spirit of togetherness and care for one another when he assigns all members of the caravan a duty in helping the ijured horse. Khru Bah is a Buddhist Monk who understands the need for peace and social justice; therefore, he trains the children to become responsible members of the society who understand the need for oneness, peace and equality. He uses the horses to bring the children from different backgrounds together (Verkerk).

Conclusion

Sulak Sivarkasa advocates for peace, social justice and equality. His oppostion to capitalism and consumerism stems from the resulting evils such as hatred, greed and delusion. He points out that Siam before the Western imperialism was a peaceful place where traditional Buddhism was respected and guided every process in the community. Due to modernization, the Siam people abandoned their traditions and emulated the western ambiguous and complex culture.

In order to ensure peace and social justice, we must rediscover the Buddhist ways of suffering, respect for nature, communism and equality. The world is plagued with struggle for power and economic gains; therefore, traditional Buddhist approach to life is the only way out of the evils facing the world.

Works Cited

Buddha's Lost Children. By Mark Verkerk. Dir. Mark Verkerk. Perf. Khru Bah. 2006.

Sivaraksa, Sulak . *Conflict, Culture, Change: Engaged Buddhism in a Globalizing World.* Somerville, MA: Wisdom Publications, 2005. Print.